REFLECTIONS
The Way I See It

WINIFRED SMITH EURE

Print information available on the last page

Rev. date: 04/25/2017

To order additional copies of this book, contact:
Xlibris
1-888-795-4274
www.Xlibris.com
Orders@Xlibris.com

For:_____

From:_____

On this _____ day of _____ _____

INTRODUCTION

When you open this book be ready to take a short journey with me where you will see, through my eyes, a few things at which I marvel. To some it may seem a bit mundane, to others spiritual, and to still others both. Put simply, it exemplifies what matters to me in this my retirement stage of my life.

As a senior citizen, I want to keep my mind active and my body moving. The former doesn't take much effort because I'm always thinking thoughts like you'll read about here; and, I like to read and hope you do too.

May your reading experience be both enlightening and enjoyable as you partake of *Reflections, The Way I See It*.

DEDICATION

This book is dedicated to my club sisters who are members of the Martin Luther King Jr. Civic Club (Members of the New Jersey State Federation of Colored Women's Clubs, Inc. & Youth Affiliates) who have been a source of stability, friendship, and love and who by virtue of being themselves, set an example of courage, responsibility and sharing.

Contents

EXCERPTS

The following are excerpts from a letter written by me (December 2016) and mailed to a Pastor who shall remain anonymous and for whom I have much respect.

I want to share my story with you. I am a 65 year old African-American Christian woman. I enjoyed a wonderful childhood, enjoying family, friends, sports and school. During my teens I experienced an unusual physical stomach illness which caused me to suffer embarrassment and depression. I finished high school and college still suffering from this illness. My parents took me to several doctors for help. Nothing helped. At the age of 40 I met a wonderful man and married him.. He accepted me as I was. However in about our 7th year of marriage he became ill. . . I tried my hardest to take care of him and continue my job as a Special Education Teacher in Newark, NJ. It became too much for me. My stepson and daughter-in-law encouraged me to have him placed in a nursing facility. I found a great Veterans home in NJ. He stayed there until he died in 2005.

Today I still suffer from gastrointestinal problems and have been diagnosed with a chemical imbalance since my late 20's. . .

I am still living in the area where I lived with my husband. This has become challenging for me and I want to move. . . I don't want to remarry. I just want to enjoy my family, friends and retirement. I belong to a women's organization, tutor in my school district and write the monthly Newsletter for my church. I am a self-published author. . .

God bless and keep you and your children, family members and congregation in His loving care.

AUTHOR'S NOTE

March 2017

It has been two months since I wrote that letter to the Pastor of my choice. Also, this is my birthday month and I have spent some time reflecting. I have decided to remain in my current home a little longer. For now it is best for me.

BLACK HISTORY THE WAY I SEE IT

B. is for the blood of our people who were slaves and often treated terribly by whippings, beatings, mutilation and branding and those who did not survive.

L. is for the lives of those slaves who found freedom after years of bondage and lives threatened today by practices of racial prejudice and discrimination.

A. is for the anointing of religious leaders who like Richard Allen saw the need for African Americans to experience religious freedom to worship God the Father, the Son and the Holy Spirit.

C. is for citizens across these United States who acknowledge the equality of the races and who stand up for justice for all.

K. is for the keeping of strong family ties to assure the foundation of African American children, to inspire them to righteous living, future leadership and the achievement of success.

H. is for hope for communities across the country who are experiencing violence and chaos in their neighborhoods.

I. is for the instilling in our youth knowledge of our rich African American heritage and culture by parents, teachers and mentors.

S. is for the sounds of music from the past and present that uplifts, inspires, and motivates our people to dance, dream and to love.

T. is for time to heal those families wounded by the loss of their loved ones who have been victims of unjust aggression and brutality by those who should know better.

O. is for opening our hearts, minds and mouths to dialogue with young people who may question and challenge rules and authority within the home and community.

R. is for the resolve to read the Bible, which is the greatest book of all times, and other literature that might cultivate our gifts and talents.

Y. is for Yes we can overcome the trials and tribulations which we face through the opposition of satanic enemies that seek to rob us of our dignity and stifle our spiritual, economic, educational and social progress.

Perfectly Made

God has made you perfectly

Perfectly made in His image

Perfectly a child of the living God

Perfectly a part of His divine plan

Perfectly assured that Jesus died for you

Perfectly sufficient in His grace

Seniors On The Move

Seniors going to the supermarket
Going to the gym
Going to see a movie
Maybe out to eat again.

Going to the casino
Going to a broadway show
Going to the mall
On a cruise for a week or so.

Going to visit children
Grands and great-grands too
Perhaps, a church or sport event
We're Seniors on the move!

Miracles

God, Jesus, Holy Spirit
Creator, Son, Comforter

A secret, a treasure, a wonder
sacred, cherished, triumphant

A dream, an idea, a seed
conceived, believed, planted

a human being, a child, a life
born, nurtured, matured

A boy, a man, a father
raised, grown, responsible

A girl, a woman, a mother
taught, loved, empowered

A measure, a time, a season
acquired, given, endured

Worship, prayer, healing
praised, petitioned, answered

Hope, faith, grace
inspired, encouraged, saved

The Word, a story, miracles
truth, lived, victory

Sistas, That's Who We Are

In Memory of Sista Joanette H. Keyes

Sistas who care
Sistas who are there

Sistas who wholeheartedly live
Sistas who unselfishly give

Sistas who love the LORD
Sistas seeking one accord

Sistas who experience trials
Sistas who resist denial

Sistas who stand and kneel
Sistas who think and feel

Sistas who have learned to cope
Sistas who don't lose hope

Sistas who build on dreams
Sistas who talk pragmatic themes

Sistas who lead
Sistas who do good deeds

Sistas who create
Sistas who know how to wait

Sistas who are mothers
Sistas who nurture others

Sistas who like to dine
Sistas who graciously shine

Sistas who are bold
Sistas young and old

Sistas who'll share o'er a cup of coffee or tea
Sistas like you and me

Mothers

Mothers are special for they
Are designed by God.

Mothers are unique.
No two are exactly alike.

Mothers are loving.
They nurture, care and protect.

Mothers are Teachers.
They lead and guide by example.

Mothers are human.
They too have flaws.

Mothers are important.
They shape and influence
Communities and the world.

Mothers are unforgettable.
The memory of them is forever
Embedded in the heart and mind.

Own Your Crown

Though you didn't earn it.
It was an act of grace
Not because of your lovely face.

Not because of the sons and daughters
to whom you gave birth
That was not the root of your worth.

Not because you stood by your man
loved hard and good
with a life in the hood

Not because your
great work brought success
your career, thought the best

Not because your
siblings and friends
coveted your wins

Not because the thorn
in your flesh
was benign, but a pest

Own Your Crown!
For the day you found Jesus
though lowly and least of us

You buried your cross
and suffered no loss.
You are Queen.

Let's Have Some Fun

My Son,
Let's have some fun.
Let's go to the park
and run, run, run.

Put down that laptop.
Turn off your cell.
Imagine you're at school
and hear the bell.

Come with Daddy.
Grab that bat!
You can make home runs
just like that.

Fly round those bases
like an eagle that soars.
Don't look back
and dream you'll hit more!

I see how you
can catch that ball.
What an outfielder you'd make!
So what if you're not tall!

Let's get the right cap,
the glove and the shoes.
And let's spread the word -
You're a player - that's news!

My Son,
We've had some fun.
It's too dark now
to continue to run.

About Love

Love holds and lets go.
It heals and it hurts.
It bends and it reaches.
It learns and it teaches.

Love gives and it takes.
It sleeps and it wakes.
It lifts and it climbs.
It seals and unwinds.

Love wins and it loses.
It silences and fuses.
It surprises and suffices.
It creates and dies.

Love surrenders and forgives.
It saves and protects.
It conquers and revives.
It's so powerful and required.

I'll Pray For You

A victim of injustice?
Bigotry and prejudice?
Yes, I'll pray for you.

Misguided and abused?
Don't know which road to choose?
Yes, I'll pray for you.

Poor in spirit and forlorn?
Wish that you were never born?
Yes, I'll pray for you.

Envying? Full of strife?
Ungrateful throughout your life?
Yes, I'll pray for you.

Whatever your story
May the end reveal God's glory.
I'll pray for you today.
For Jesus has spoken. He is the way.

Let It Be Lord

Let me heal, Lord.
Let me live.
Let me wait, Lord.
Let me give.

Let me learn, Lord.
Let me be free.
Let me stand, Lord.
Let my heart and soul agree.

Let me abide, Lord
Your spirit always within.
Let me grow in faith, Lord
Your adoration to win.

Let me never forsake, Lord
The trust I have in thee.
Let me keep on praying, Lord
'les Satan conquer me.

Let me honor your precepts, Lord
Today and forevermore.
Your name, your glory
Let me endlessly adore!
Amen.

Where Do We Go From Here?

Where do we go from here?
Are you lonely?
Are you sad, My Dear?

The uncertainty of tomorrow
The regrets of yesterday
The here and now of today that follows.

Where do we go from here?
I see you in my dreams
When will you appear?

Your touch was so redundant.
Your face ever aglow
Your giving always abundant.

Where do we go from here?
I count it all joy
You are genuinely sincere.

Morning, afternoon and evening
I think of you
Will you remain or are you leaving?

Where do we go from here?
Should I anticipate a smile
Or will there be a tear?

Somehow I knew the answer.
'Twas not the forest, but a tree
Reality did occur.

You, My Love, are free.

My Loss, My Gain

His mind had lost its sharpness.
His hair began to thin.
His gait, somewhat unsteady.
He seemed quite pitiful then.

Reminiscing, he thought of all the old,
familiar places he had been in his life.
He sat down and talked to God.
How I miss my wife!

Why did You have to take her?
What she not a gift of grace?
I miss her words. I miss her smile.
Her beautiful brown face.

My days and night seem oh so long.
The years, without their charm.
Keep me. Guide me, Heavenly Father
Away from Satan's harm.

You must have heard my plea and prayer
For one day in the city
I met a girl. Her name was Nell.
And she was even pretty.

My hope is that we become good friends
as days and months go by.
I need a wife in my life
before my time to die.

That's Life!

Life is a heartbeat.
Life is a tale.
Life is a journey
to walk with victory and to fail.

Life is a measure of time.
Life is a choice.
Life is a circumstance.
Life is a voice.

Life is a battle.
Life is a test.
Life is a way to be.
Life's our worst and best.

Life is a gift.
Life is a song.
Life is a dream come true.
Life is right and wrong.

Life is a garden.
Life is a sea.
Life is a desert.
Life's a growing and grown-up tree.

When He Arose

When He arose we understood
He died not only for our sin,
but to set us on a lifetime path of
repentance from within.

When He arose it did not mean
that we would not have sorrow,
but the joy of knowing how much he loves us
would sustain us each tomorrow.

When He arose
Our Jesus renewed our hope and faith.
He gave us the blessed assurance
that we could win this race

that goes not to the swift or strong
proud women, youth, or men,
but to His precious, undeserving ones
that endure to the end.

All The Way Home

One day I'm going
all the way home
having traveled from my youth
to the grace of God's throne.

Days of innocence and trust
Days of awkwardness and plus
guilty stains

One day I'm going
all the way home
far from the silence
of living alone.

There to be with
my Heavenly Father.

Days of pride
and days of grief
days of joy and sweet relief

One day I'm going
all the way home.
I'll say a prayer
and write my last poem.

Days of promise
and regret
Days of not understanding yet

One day I'm going
all the way home -
heir to His kingdom, Atoned!

Have You Lived Well?

Have you lived well?
Done most of those things
you've wanted to do? BUT
Have you given your life to Christ
who one day rescued you?

Have you lived well?
Traveled some roads to success?
BUT Are you living thankful that you
have been Heavenly blessed?

Have you lived well?
You say you own some silver and gold?
BUT Are you a Christian
who is faithful and bold?

Have you lived well?
Got that house on a hill?
Do you know it was Jesus that
paid the bill?

Have you lived well?
One hundred friends, one hundred stories?
Can this compare to the Bible
and its contents of God's glory?

Have you lived well?
Loved your children and spouse?
Would Jesus be welcome anytime
in your house?

If you have lived well
It's a fact oh so true.
The Lord God Almighty
Has His hands on you.

Photo By: Calvin W. Robinson

Printed in the United States
By Bookmasters